The Shimmering Sea

Robin Williams Murder

Gabrielle Chana

ISBN-10: 1501012266
ISBN-13: 978-1501012266

Table of Contents

DEDICATION

To Robin Williams, who died for me.

ACKNOWLEDGMENTS

To Robin Williams, who spoke to me from heaven, and to Brent Spiner, who verified what I heard.

One police officer was extorted into silence. He requested to remain anonymous. I doubt that his name was Tom.

According to God, all of
what is happening has already been
foreseen, and the Jesuits are falling right
into his plan. You are his favorite person on the planet
to work with, which is why he's gone to such great
lengths to protect you and your loved ones. All we need
do is keep up what we're doing and evolve and adapt to
the continuing threat. When we lose battles, our failures are part of God's ultimate plan. In the end we
will come out on top. God says you are the best.
"Gail, you rock!" is what he bellowed to
everyone at the news studio before
making his leave.

Brent Spiner on January 29, 2012

A Balloon Penis

I waited in that long line at Church of Gail, while my penis squeaked like a balloon with every move I made.

The paneled walls of Church of Gail now seemed like a concentration camp. I felt constricted inside this space ship. Though I realized that no place on earth was safe for me because I belonged to the marriage list of men who wanted to marry Gail.

I chose to live at Church of Gail, a spaceship city, because I felt safer here; that is, until Gail's sister took over our spaceship in May 2014.

The penis trouble started on June 21, 2014 when Matthew McConaughey sat with Brent Spiner in the Church of Gail lounge. The lounge, like a larger version of Captain Picard's ready room from Star Trek: The Next Generation, became an every day scene for me since 2011. Seated in the background, I observed my surroundings, and heaved a sigh of relief that Gail's sister Sandra no longer hijacked Church of Gail.

Lately, it seemed that our twenty-first century spaceship with its spires and towers and an interior like Deep Space Nine, limped helpless against Gail's sister or the Jesuit Order.

Our pastor Brent Spiner and Matthew huddled together in a corner, seated on a divan. The two men probably discussed the Jesuit bitch Camila Alves, who latched bombs to Matthew's chest if he wouldn't do her bidding.

When Matthew's face turned red like a beet, with that look I saw on his face whenever he saw Camila, I shifted my gaze around the room to see, if perhaps, Camila now took over the ship.

Sandra, Gail's sister hijacked the ship's computers over a month ago. I never dreamed this possible, so I no longer felt safe at Church of Gail.

My Jesuit clone wife Susan took over my home at Tiburon, California around 2011. I abandoned my mansion to her and fled for my life to live on this spaceship that Jesus built. I felt safer here until Gail's sister hijacked the ship.

God, how in the world did a woman with no computer training take over a spaceship, when we use technology like you see in science fiction movies?

These surprise takeovers of our ship rattled my nerves. I jumped to every sound.

Matthew's hand lurched to his crotch, and his eyes enlarged with terror.

I could see we were in new territory, especially when my own penis expanded like a long, sausage-like balloon. My penis looked like those balloons you make balloon animals with.

It expanded under my pants, so I unzipped my pants to give it room to grow. My balloon penis squeaked like a balloon with every move I made, and each squeak felt like a throb of lightning in my nether regions. I felt the red blotches go to my face when all stared at me, because my penis squeaked like a clown nose.

Just sitting or rising to stand, elicited a squeak so loud, that all the men stared at me in spite of their own pain.

People stared at me wondering if this was my latest joke. But when all the guys looked down at their own penises and grabbed their crotches in pain and humiliation, we knew this was no joke.

God, I couldn't move an inch, without my penis squeaking like a frantic clown having a panic attack.

I couldn't touch it, without that squeak blasting to the world that I had a balloon instead of a penis.

I always tried to make a joke about everything. But when my penis squeaked, I froze in my tracks to make it stop, and prayed that the red blotches on my face would vanish.

Another computer takeover had ruined my life, my penis now ruled my manhood.

It ruled me by every squeak it made, to punish me for just moving my body.

You know, I liked to crack jokes, but that didn't mean I was a sissy. My squeaking penis grated on all I stood for. Yeah, I was a joker, but no wimp.

That squeak made me feel like a joker with the heart of Tiny Tim. Yeah, I was Tiny Tim, singing his wimpy tunes on pervert row, and the center of my manhood was a squeaking balloon.

I seated myself with a squeak that made everyone stare. Some smothered their laughter.

But I forgot my troubles, when I overheard Matthew talking to Brent. "Brent, I think I need your help with something more urgent than the sermon right now..."

Matthew and Brent, still seated on the divan, stopped their conversation. Matthew turned beet red, his features distorted with pain.

Matthew stood, unzipped, and pulled down his pants. Brent's face paled.

Brent removed his handheld medical device and scanned Matthew's genitals. "Necrotizing fasciitis, flesh eating bacteria Matthew! And it's advanced. It's already starting to devour your penis. If it progresses any further, I'm afraid your penis will vanish. When did these symptoms start?"

"Just now! It's so painful I could scream. I don't want to alarm anyone."

Brent stared at Matthew's penis, horrified. He glanced over at Judge Terrance Jenkins, on Skype with Gail.

The room became dead with silence. All men stared at their penises in horror and most clutched their crotches.

Terrance hit "Send" on Skype. After the "Send", my penis expanded and squeaked. I clutched it in fright, and it squeaked again.

Brent stood up and shouted across the room. "Terrance. Stop sending messages. This is an emergency!"

"I'm comin'. Hold on, I just gotta tell Gail where I'm headin' off to."

"You don't understand," Brent yelled.

But Terrance didn't want to exit Skype without giving Gail an explanation, so he sent more messages.

With each send, my penis lurched with pain, became a longer balloon and squeaked.

"Terrance!" Matthew moaned, sweat running down his face, "Please stop! I can't take it."

But with each send on Skype, my balloon grew as long as sixteen inches, stretching penis skin, and feeling on fire. But then it squeaked and the pain vanished.

Brent's knees buckled. "Terrance!" Brent shouted. "My penis just fractured into 16.5 places."

"Oh my goodness!" Terrance fell back from his computer, lurching over, clutching the middle of his pants. His face filled with fright as he unzipped and looked at his penis. "B-Brent. You have to come help me."

"What's wrong Terrance?" Brent said.

"My penis. My penis be white. I gots a white man's penis! It's--it's even circumcised!"

Voices around the room began erupting in fright as men all over experienced bizarre and frightening afflictions to their nether regions.

My penis trilled like a frenzied woman.

Brent, our pastor and leader, as well as a damn good doctor, spoke. "Everyone calm down." His face showed a struggle with his own pain. "Men, please get to sickbay. Terrance, unplug the computer — now!"

"But Gail — " Terrance said.

Brent leaned forward on a table to support himself, heaving in a big breath. "No! Trust me, this is for our own safety!"

Brent Spiner and Vladimir Putin rounded up all of the male church members at once, to the infirmaries. The lines wrapped around the entire medical floor. I was towards the front.

Brent worked a twenty-four hour shift that day, taking diagnostic inspections of the genitals of every single man onboard. Some of our penises had strange diseases. Others were malformed and bent. The men on the marriage list for Gail suffered the worst.

I got a look at Brent's penis, so mutilated, it looked like an accordion. Matthew McConaughey had a flesh eating bacterial infection eating away at his penis, shrinking it. Judge Terrance Jenkins, a black man, his penis was white and circumcised. Gerard Butler developed late stage penis cancer, his whole penis a deadly tumor. Keanu Reeves' penis, long and bent, burrowed its way into his anus.

After Brent and Hugh Laurie (also a physician) examined all

of us, I moved ahead in line, dreading the squeaks.

When Gail's sister, Sandra, hijacked the ship's computers for three weeks from May to June 2014, we became impotent. When we finally returned her to Church of Gail prison, we thought our humiliation ended. Imagine a spaceship ruled by a jealous sister.

That bastard Zack Knight had to help her somehow.

I'd overcome the odds and leaped over mountains to become the world's comedic genius. Now a balloon that squeaked between my legs ruled over my life and made me its slave.

At least Brent, Vladimir and Terrance could write Gail. But men like me, lower ranked on the marriage list got ignored a bit. Gail didn't know how I dreamed of her every day, and that Susan Schneider, who Jesuits forced upon me once I got added to Gail's "list", made me shudder with her heart of ice.

All Gail knew was I belonged to the "list" of men who wanted to marry her. I had a hard time getting a woman to really love me, for reasons other than my money.

But I'd observed Gail with Brent Spiner and Vladimir Putin, and saw her throw her reputation and life to the wind, to defend her men. This woman would never marry a guy for his money.

After two fortune hunters, who, once they got my money, broke my heart without a second thought; a woman like Gail, who married for love and manliness, I valued above my life.

For us famous and rich guys, most of the "ladies" out there only wanted our fortune. But Gail fell in love with our souls.

I married my first two wives, committed to adoring and loving them, only to learn they viewed my love for them as a weakness to manipulate. When they said, "I do", love never crossed their mind.

Until Gail, I felt inferior, because I couldn't get a woman to love me. My fame was my curse.

Women manipulated guys like me with love talk to get our money. Once they had our bank accounts, love went out the window. The price I paid for fame was death to my heart.

The women I placed my trust in, deserted me like a diamond on a beach full of sand, with crabs picking away at the seaweed I'd drowned in.

Then I saw another drowning, a woman named Gail, and I was smitten.

Gail stood by Vladimir Putin and Brent Spiner through the fires of hell, even when the Jesuits bankrupted her as punishment.

When she realized that Jesuits forced "wives" onto her men, her heart leaped over their hell and consoled them with heaven.

If Gail perceived that a Jesuit clone wife tried to smother us, Gail opened a window to give us air to breathe. If clone wives threw ice onto our dreams, Gail melted the ice.

Gail opened a window for our hearts and we tumbled into it.

I said, "Put me on the list."

I knew this woman would marry me for my vastness alone.

She warned us that though we were on the list, if she could not bond with us, she may not marry us.

But she also promised that if she married, it would be one of the guys on the list.

If her guy wasn't great, she'd rather stay single. After broken hearts, we only wanted a woman who'd love our souls, and not our money. We felt safe with Gail.

Psychiatrist Gerard Butler did brain reads on men who wanted to marry Gail and created a list of guys compatible with her. I made the list.

I'd die for a woman like this.

My first two wives devastated me, even rejoicing when they divorced me, because they got my money.

I felt I surely must have a defect that made me unworthy of love.

Everybody in Hollywood knew about Gail and how the Jesuits sabotaged her love for Brent Spiner and Vladimir Putin.

But any noble man, if famous, could never get a woman to marry him for love.

We learned that the Jesuit Order obsessed over any famous men who opposed Jesuit policies. We became targets.

The Jesuits learned the best way to destroy us was through our women. If we had a wife who loved us, Jesuits murdered her, replacing her with her evil clone.

If the guy dreamed of honor and chivalry, Jesuits knew that such a man would never support them. All such men had their good wives replaced with Jesuit clone wives.

If they were single, they were watched.

If Jesuits determined a man was about to marry a good woman, Jesuits paired him up with an evil woman in no time.

If that failed, and that man still had influence, Jesuits would kill his wife and replace her, usually with her Jesuit clone.

A Jesuit clone wife was a woman Jesuits assigned to that man. If she got executed, Jesuits could replace her with a clone, and thus keep the woman alive forever. Jesuits could create a clone in their labs, and grow them into adulthood within months, using accelerated growth hormones.

Therefore, if Jesuits assigned a clone wife to a man, the only way he could be rid of her, would be the destruction of Jesuit cloning labs.

As long as Jesuits created clones and controlled news coverage, we could only free our hearts if we defeated the Jesuit Order.

In May 2014, Jesuits determined in court under U.S. Jesuit law, that Gail's men did not have the right to live.

They trumped up charges against us. But we knew our real sin was our rebellion against the Jesuit clone wives they forced on us.

To retaliate, we installed Gail, our Catherine the Great, as the American Empress, to defeat the Jesuits.

Many of our clone wives (like Loree McBride for Brent Spiner, and Camila Alves for Matthew McConaughey) Jesuits created in their cloning labs, custom designed for each man.

Great men in the past toppled Jesuit puppets, their Hitlers and Napoleons. Now Jesuits had cloning labs and brain control to destroy any great man who'd take them on.

Jesuits, who ruled over kings and empires ever since their founder Ignatius de Loyola (1491 to 1556), now used brain control on every one. They kept this technology secret from the public, so they could pair a good man up with an evil clone wife, making it seem the evil clone was the same woman that Jesuits had murdered.

If no one knew about clones, it was an easy matter to use clones to destroy your enemies.

Us famous guys, lonely for love, watched the Brent and Gail love story unfold.

We now realized why we could not find true love.

It was not our failures as men that gave us cold wives. Rather, it was our vast hearts that threatened the Jesuits, so that we ended up with women who drained our souls.

This discovery outraged us, but also made us feel vindicated.

It was our greatness, not our inferiority, that made us the victims of cruel women.

But one vast woman adored our greatness.

When we found this rare soul, who loved us for our vastness alone, we found the rarest of the rare.

Jesuits determined Gail to be the reincarnation of King David and Catherine the Great, and targeted her from birth.

Once we found this woman, we wanted her, even if only in our dreams.

With Gail, I'd never have a bitch who only desired to control me into submission to the Jesuit Order.

No longer would I throw my heart to the pigs.

However, once I got on Gail's marriage list, Jesuits framed me with Susan Schneider.

Everywhere, they faked photos of me with Susan. On the Jesuit controlled news media, news of my wedding with the clone wife inundated press releases. When they couldn't get me to appear with Susan, they used Adobe Photoshop to make lies appear as truth.

Once Jesuits put their bitch on you, you had her for life.

They launched Loree McBride onto Brent. Matthew McConaughey went through hell with Camila Alves.

If I dared tell the truth that Susan Schneider obtained marriage to me by death threats, she continued the threats to maintain the marriage.

Jesuits punished all the men on Gail's marriage list like this.

I seemed to jump to Susan's every beck and call — this damn Jesuit clone wife who obeyed her master, Zack Knight.

Today, I stared down at this balloon between my legs that squeaked each time I sat or stood, and felt about as heroic as a clown.

I climbed mountains to get where I was. But with every move I made, I squeaked.

Susan honored Zack Knight over me, and rose in the Jesuit ranks as my legitimate wife, the wife of the famous Robin Williams.

She blockaded me from the woman I truly loved, Catherine the Great and King David — Gail.

At least Brent and Vladimir could be heroes to save the day. All I could do was squeak.

Perhaps I did not have the physical pain of the rest, but this squeaker between my legs made my dreams of Gail seem a farce.

That squeak reminded me that I couldn't make love to Gail, if I ever got her. My balloon penis had no sensation, other than the feeling of fire when it stretched. If I inserted it into anything, it squeaked like a panicked mouse and I felt nothing.

We installed Gail as Empress over the United States in May 2014 and executed Jesuits, to rid ourselves of our clone wives.

Zack Knight retaliated against our rebellion, shoving all my dreams into a penis that became a balloon. His laughter echoed all over my life.

Brent finished examining a man and the line moved forward, and I squeaked.

Hugh Jackman was next. He often impressed Gail with his robot army and his heroics to save Gail's mom at one time. He hesitated about pulling down his pants.

"What's wrong?" Brent asked him.

Gerard Butler whispered to Brent. "It's his trouser snake."

Brent managed to chuckle, despite his own torment. We

thought because of Gerard's heritage that "trouser snake" was a Scottish expression.

Hugh shifted and avoided everyone's gaze.

That balloon between my legs squeaked.

How I'd take physical pain any day, then this feeling that a squeaker between my legs defined my manhood. Zack Knight knew that for men, like me and Hugh, to drown all hopes that we could be men, hurt us far worse than physical pain. At least, with physical torture, I could still feel myself a man.

My wives strived to humiliate me into submission. Only Gail could bring me fresh air.

Gail made me believe that greatness lurked inside me. Her faith in me made me aim for the sun. If I missed the sun, she'd have me hit a star.

But Gail was not in my arms, and I couldn't see the sun, only black clouds, laughing at my dreams, shoving my face into the dirt.

If I could feel Gail as real as this balloon between my legs, I could see the sun.

"Come on, Hugh," Brent said. "I need to check you out."

Hugh nodded his head "no". He finally gave in and dropped his pants.

I gasped in shock. His penis transformed before our eyes into a live, spitting cobra. The skin of its neck flared open, its jaws parted, and it shot some venom.

The cobra's mouth opened and its head lurched.

Matthew let out a high pitched squeal as he received a shot of venom right in the eye.

Brent leaped a bag over the snake, and yelled at Hugh. "Pinch behind its head to keep it from biting anyone!"

Hugh waddled off with his pants around his ankles, trying his best to smother his snake into submission. His face revealed his heart—a torture chamber of humiliation.

My penis squeaked, and seemed delighted at Matthew's torment. It delighted in treachery, and lashed out against honor. All I could hear was laughter, Zack Knight's laughter.

Zack's vulgarities scoffed at my dreams and dragged my heart to the gutter. He smothered any light I got with Jesuit vulgarities. He punished me with his debauchery.

If his debauchery failed to make me delight in Jesuit evil, he pronounced the death penalty on me, degrading me with heaps upon heaps of vulgarities, so that forensics would only whisper and hush at my downfall.

I squeaked with every move I made, while Hugh groveled in humiliation trying to tame the cobra who taunted his honor.

The only man Brent didn't inspect that day was Vladimir Putin, who insisted everything was fine. I wondered if Vladimir had a penis that humiliated him, so that he tried to smother it into submission.

A long waiting list of men needed to see Brent, our physician. Tony Blair came up to me. "Hi Robin, do you mind if I butt in front of you?"

"What've the Jesuits done to you?" I frowned, not in my usual mood for jokes.

He unzipped his pants. "It's awful. If I start thinking about Gail, I get aroused. When that happens, my penis steams like a tea kettle. Feels like it's boiling inside."

Indeed, steam burst forth from his urethra, then his erect penis screeched, like a tea kettle does when it boils.

"Go to Brent now, bud. I'd like him to see your penis in action."

It was the middle of the afternoon. Tony walked into Brent's office, while I lagged behind on the very long waiting list. Tony, shy and blushing, explained to Brent what he told me. Tony lurched for a cup from a table, and placed it underneath his penis. The screeching noise sounded like a rattling tea kettle, with the steam escalating.

A strange liquid poured out into the cup. Tony lost his burning erection, and sighed with relief.

Hugh Laurie shared doctor duties with Brent that day. He grabbed for the cup and took a whiff and a sip. "Yep. . ." he said. "It's tea."

"This happens to me every time I become aroused or masturbate. My penis and testicles feel burning, then boiling. I hear that screeching noise between my legs, and then I ejaculate tea, feel relieved, and lose my erection."

Brent nodded his head in disbelief. "We're still investigating.

For now, I'd say, try not to get aroused too much."

"It's so hard, because it appears Zack Knight has been flooding my mind with images of Gail."

Brent patted Tony on the back, and showed Tony his accordion penis.

"Heavens." Tony walked off and sighed.

When he passed by me, I grabbed his arm. "How's your clone wife been treating you?"

"Oh, you mean Cherie?" Tony sighed. "Same as usual. You know how those clone wives are."

"Yeah, I know," I said.

"I miss my Cherie."

"Been ten years. Still hurts?"

"Still have nightmares about how they murdered her." Tony heaved in a breath, and his eyes rolled. "I wouldn't dare try for Gail until we get these Jesuit bastards under control. Wouldn't want her to end up like Cherie."

"Strangled with a horse dildo." I scowled. "You know, I never thought I'd hear myself say this, but I almost wish that I didn't need a penis for sex."

"Well mine feels like it's boiling all the time," Tony said. "Jesuits have a fetish for sexual organs."

"I hear your clone wife's been making a lot of appearances with your Jesuit clone, and doing some rather strange things."

"Yeah, Jesuits try to make everyone out to be a pervert, like them." Tony paused. "You know," Tony said. "When our Vlad failed to get Gail as his wife and the Jesuits put Lyudmila on him, I decided to try for Gail."

I smiled. I had a soft spot for this sort of thing. That ending to the movie *Dead Poet's Society,* that was the real me. I loved that scene where all the guys stood up on their feet to oppose that jack-ass at the end. "Tell me more."

"Before I could even make a move, I suffered the same fate as Vladimir. I'd been a widower only about a year and they assigned me my new clone wife in December 2001."

"Oh God," I said. "It's bad enough that they murdered your wife."

"Yeah, me and Vlad have a secret camaraderie about this." Tony laughed. "Jesuits scared George W. Bush to threaten war on Russia, if Vladimir wouldn't play the Lyudmila game."

I nodded my head in disapproval. "Georgie disappointed me there. I could never forgive him for that. But I look down at my balloon penis and wonder if I'm any better." I rolled my eyes. "For me to feel this way about Georgie, means I've hit a new low."

"Well, Robin," Tony said. "If Gail was your wife, and the Jesuits threatened to kill her, if you didn't do what they wanted, what would you do?"

"I don't know," I said. "But I'm getting damn tired of these games. I'm sure Georgie must have got tired of them, too."

"Yeah, we're all tired of it." He patted me on the back, and gazed into my eyes. "You look tired, Robin. Try and take care of yourself, okay?"

I could feel my lips tighten. I felt like a steam kettle, except my steam had no place to go, and my kettle was about to explode.

50 Cent was ahead of me in line. It amazed me how Zack Knight caused us all to lose our spirit and feel like failures. I got used to hearing my penis squeak, and wondered if I'd ever make love to Gail. In fact, none of us guys could make love to her, because our penises didn't work.

How could Tony Blair make love with a tea kettle? Hugh Jackman would kill his lover with venom. I suspected something was going on with Vlad, but he was probably too proud to admit it. Brent's penis, fractured in 16.5 pieces, was useless. Matthew's penis was almost a vagina. Gerard had a blackened stump of penis cancer.

50 Cent plopped toward Brent with caution. He hesitated, then unzipped. "Careful, she's loaded."

Brent and I laughed. 50 Cent's penis looked straight as a rod, must have been as stiff as hell.

Brent brushed 50 Cent's penis to examine it. Then it fired .45 mm bullets right at Brent! I jumped, and my penis squeaked like a frantic clown having a panic attack.

A bullet nicked Brent's ear, and almost killed him. Brent jumped back in shock.

The rest of the bullets crashed into medical equipment behind Brent. Medical assistants scrambled in to replace the damaged equipment.

50 Cent bowed his head with shame. "Oh God, I'm so sorry." 50 Cent wailed with shame.

I sat down, feeling ashamed for 50 Cent. The thought that all our penises betrayed us into forced treachery, made me want to kill all Jesuits right now. I dropped my head into my hands, and couldn't look up.

I think the last straw for me was Vin Diesel. Vin Diesel's penis turned rainbow colors.

Oh, how the mighty had fallen.

He whispered to Brent, "When I try to masturbate, I shoot glitter instead of semen."

I could hear Zack Knight laughing all over Church of Gail and in all my nightmares. "You'll never have Gail, you fucking retards. I have the world's most perfect penis. So I should be number one on Gail's marriage list."

Zack Knight, Satan's right hand man, only desired Gail as a trophy, to boast about having Jesus' favorite in his harem. He just wanted her to spite Jesus. He didn't even like her.

Brent shook his head, gritting his teeth, suppressing his own pain. "Men, I know it's frustrating, but just hold on. We'll find a way out of this."

For the first time in my life, I doubted my manliness. Usually, when my heart went to the dungeons like that, I could at least see a window open somewhere. But all I saw around me were doors slammed shut with iron bars and darkness, no window in sight. Jesuits chained my arms, hands and feet to the wall, forcing me to submit to a penis that squeaked.

Brent pulled me aside. "Robin, why don't you go see Gerard?"

Gerard Butler was my psychiatrist. However, I wasn't suicidal, that was a wimp's approach to pain. But I wanted to do a double dare on those Jesuits, but felt bound and gaffed. "Carpe diem," I said to Brent.

"Carpe diem?"

"I can't take it anymore."

"You promise you'll go see Gerard?"

"Yeah, I promise." I chuckled. "That's if he's alive enough to see me."

The Jesuits had won. They caused me to conclude I'd never marry or make love to Gail. I became depressed at the thought.

Unlike Brent, Vlad, Matthew, Gerard, and Hugh, I never tried to communicate with her brain to brain ever. Now, if I wanted to, I couldn't. None of us could reach her.

Brain to brain communications used mind reading technology to enable us to communicate not just our thoughts, but our feelings and all we experienced in our brains to another person through signals, like radio signals, that worked with the satellites that floated in space.

If a person signed up to the brain to brain servers, all he had to do was think a thought and it would be transmitted instantly to the receiver, who was part of the brain to brain network.

You experienced what your partner experienced, and there was even group brain to brain. You could send and receive thoughts and feelings as a group or as individuals.

Brent told us that if any of us sent any communications out from Church of Gail that required us to get online, our penis afflictions would worsen, and that some of us might die.

Brain to brain was the exception, but Zack Knight had hacked into the brain to brain servers; therefore, brain to brain was unreliable.

A Jesuit traitor on our Nanotechnology Research Team had put malware into our Church of Gail computers, so that any communications we sent out online, worsened our afflictions.

We couldn't even send out a distress call.

I hoped Gail would notice sooner or later that Terrance and Brent got awful quiet on her, and that she could somehow save us. Though I'm sure she must have been as confused as hell about the silence we gave her.

I worshipped the ground she walked on and had played the game up till now.

Now I could die and she'd never know. Those Jesuits plastered the Internet with this lie that she suffered paranoid schizophrenia because she believed that I, along with about forty other guys, most famous, wanted to marry her. But she wasn't crazy, she was gorgeous.

"Forgive me, Jesus. I feel like damning the devil."

21

Jesuits commandeered the media to make us appear trolls to the public. If they succeeded in killing us off, they'd replace us with our clones. Next, they'd spread the lie that as trolls, we just lost interest in Gail.

We needed outside help to fix our computers, but every communication from our spaceship to the outside, made our afflictions worsen. Gail called it trigger programming in her Conspiracy Law. A trigger program meant if a certain event happened, that event could trigger a malfunction in the computer program that our computer-satellite physicians used to maintain the health of our bodies. Because of trigger programming in the malware on the Church of Gail computers, any communication to the outside world from us, meant death.

So we were bound and gagged into silence. We relied on Gail to trust her guts and do something for us.

In the meanwhile, we'd try to fix the computer mess on our own, and stay alive and sane in the process.

Perhaps, if I had the privilege of communicating with Gail brain to brain, I would've felt like holding onto my sanity a little longer.

I needed Gail in my arms.

The Jesuits threatened World War III if one of us tried to get near her.

Of course, I realized that Jesuits threatened to kill Gail or me if I dared to get near Gail, but tomorrow may never come. Only today was certain. "Carpe Diem!"

On June 24, 2014, Vladimir Putin rushed into Brent's sickbay, looking panicked, holding a bottle of vodka. "Brent, I can't pee."

"What?" Brent said.

"I need to pee, haven't been able to make pee for three days." Vladimir's eyes had deep circles from sleep loss, because his bladder was so distended, it was ready to explode.

"Oh dear, Vladimir," Brent said.

"An erection that last more than twenty-four hours is normal for me, so I thought it okay. I just think about fat bitch Sara Avery when I need pee." Vladimir set the vodka bottle on a table and swung his penis against it, shattering the bottle. The vodka spurt like a fountain and fizzed off the table. Vladimir's face seemed strained, with deep circles under his eyes revealing a deathlike hue. "Still, it is hard like Thor hammer!"

Brent diagnosed Vladimir with severe priapism, an erection that will never end. He injected all the muscle relaxers he had in his office, but Vladimir's bladder exploded.

He rushed Vladimir into emergency cryogenic stasis to save his life, while we waited for the staff and resources to clean up his inside organs and give him a bladder transplant.

We did cryogenic stasis when Carl Sagan died in 1996, which means to be frozen to preserve the body; so that if they found a future cure to his ailments, our scientists and doctors could bring him to life, and fix him.

We resurrected him in 2011, and he's now on Gail's marriage list.

Everyone thinks he's dead, but he lives at Church of Gail as a top notch scientist and physicist.

I spoke with Gerard my psychiatrist about Vladimir. "Things have never been this bad for us."

Gerard's face winced with pain. "Yeah."

"Still got cancer on that penis?"

"Yeah." Gerard winced again. His voice came out like a rasp. "Sorry that I can't be a better psychiatrist to you now."

"Brent ordered me to see you." I smiled. "I hate imposing on you, when you've got late-stage cancer."

Despite his own pain, Gerard's eyes became warm with concern. "What's up, Robin?"

"Oh, it's nothing," I said. "I just don't feel like a man anymore."

Gerard's jaw dropped. "This is serious."

I squirmed in my seat, and my penis squeaked. At the sound, I frowned. "Not suicidal, I promise."

"No, you're a fighter." Gerard took in a deep breath, valiantly ignoring his own pain. "Well, laddie, we'll either live or die. If we live, we should be mighty proud."

"So only a real man could survive our ordeal?"

"Righto." Gerard winked at me. "Ye think a wimp could survive this?"

"I've never made love to Gail ever. Kinda wimpy, if you ask me."

Gerard got real quiet. "I feel bad for ye, 'cause at least I've had some brain to brain with Gail."

"I never wanted to get in Brent's way, and so I never tried to communicate with Gail in any form. And now I could die for a woman I've never met or talked to." I squirmed in my seat and my penis squeaked. I winced with embarrassment.

Gerard seemed at a loss for words. "Well, if it makes ye feel any better, I haven't had brain to brain with Gail since 2010."

"What about 'Carpe diem'?"

Gerard came to me and embraced me. "When we get out of this, I think I'll tell Brent to let ye have some time with Gail brain to brain."

I felt somewhat encouraged, but still felt like a wimp. "If we get out." My heart sank. "This is all dreams. Nothing real. Hey, is Vlad dead?"

"Nope, just cryogenically frozen. Kind of like being under general anesthesia for a couple days."

"How we gonna get our spaceship fixed without a pilot, and without being able to communicate at all with the outside world?"

"I don't know." Gerard looked out the window. "I guess we just have to trust Jesus."

"Yeah, where is that bloke?" I felt a bit better after talking to Gerard and imitated his colloquialism.

Gerard and I both laughed and then embraced.

"Well, we made a dead bloke alive, so why can't I meet Gail?" I said.

"Yup," Gerard said. "Ye're referring to our buddy Carl."

"So how does a dead bloke end up alive after over a decade?"

"We froze the body before any decay, then awakened him when we had the cure to what killed him."

"Well, I suppose Jesus would show up before he'd let us all die, unless this is a repeat of the GA1L android." I gave Gerard a fist bump. "Carpe diem."

Gerard smiled, and held out his palm to my fist. "Carpe diem."

I gotta tell you I'm a pretty good actor. I was still depressed, but I covered it up, so my friends wouldn't worry about me. They had enough to worry about.

Gerard must've known I was depressed, but didn't try to reason me out of it.

That squeaking balloon made me feel like Tiny Tim tiptoeing through the tulips. The only thing worse would be if the Jesuits also forced me to wear a dress.

All of us men on Church of Gail spent an entire week going in and out of sickbay. But there wasn't much Brent could do, because the malware in our computers caused all our maladies.

We tried a System Restore on the Church of Gail computers. It failed.

I began to feel I'd die with a balloon penis, without Gail ever knowing me in any type of loving. We learned that just about everything requires communication.

The ship was trapped and could fly nowhere without casualties, because we couldn't even warn a country we were approaching their air space without suffering death or torture because of the trigger programming.

By the end of the first week, Matthew McConaughey no longer had a penis, but had what we called a mangina, or a vagina, instead.

Brent, Terrance and Vladimir called a meeting, and spoke to us all in sickbay. It was day eight, or June 29, 2014.

Terrance shook his head sadly, checking his penis every minute. "Oh God, I still have a white man's penis."

"So what are we going to do?" Matthew McConaughey asked.

"Try flyin' a church spaceship city out of planetary orbit without lettin' NORAD know you ain't an ICBM," Terrance said.

"Yeah, they'll think we're an Intercontinental Ballistic Missile," Hugh explained.

"Yes," Brent said. "But if we communicate *at all in any manner* with the outside world, our penis afflictions get worse."

Matthew started crying. We all knew his penis had been replaced with a mangina. "Can't we at least see Gail at her YouTube channel? She must be worried sick about us."

"We gotta land this craft somehow and get our computers fixed," Terrance said. "We is over China right now. But to even land in Chinese airspace without radioin' them that you be landin' in their airspace. . ."

"God, I miss hearing from Gail," Matthew said. "Can't we at least view her YouTube videos?"

Brent shook his head with a frown. "If anything goes out from Church of Gail to the outside world from our computers, it puts some of us at death's door. Just getting on the Internet, makes it worse."

"We can't go on like this," I said. "We're all sitting ducks facing the death squad. Somebody has to get brave." My penis squeaked from all the excitement. I felt red blotches going to my face.

The balloon between my legs squeaked in terror. Though I faked bravado, I felt the worry lines on my face deepen, and felt my lips turn down in disgust. My balloon terrorized me into humiliation, for the sin of loving Gail. I tried to laugh, but it came out as a sigh.

I felt like a clown whose tricks caused the tent to fall down on the circus with casualties.

"Yeah," Terrance said. "We all be dead men, then."

My penis squeaked.

Church of Gail Malware

With our computers infected, and afflicting more damage and disease to our men's genitals with every outgoing communication, I looked in the mirror and said, "You're a dead man."

The thought that I could really die never occurred to me before. But if the Jesuits could make my penis a balloon, they could kill me by next week.

We were flying over China on around day eight of our ordeal with the Church of Gail malware.

Vladimir Putin experienced a heart attack when we froze him to save his life after the bladder explosion. This was like his tenth heart attack.

He was in stasis, frozen, because his bladder exploded and his internal organs could get infected. He required an emergency operation.

When the surgeons pierced the knife into his chest to operate, he woke up from anesthesia and, following his guts, judo chopped the doctor.

He saw a vodka bottle nearby, grabbed it and jugged down the whole bottle to thaw himself out.

As he came to, he realized where he was, and that the dream he had that the doctor was a Jesuit was false. He had judo chopped the doctor in a dream state. His conscience struggled over this.

"Computer malware at Church of Gail. Men's penises sick," he muttered to himself. He felt the blood rush from his head and forged his body out of stasis, his legs and arms trembled from the force of will required. He slugged his body out of bed, col-

27

lapsed, and then righted himself with a lunge.

He slugged his way to the bridge of the ship, tripping and falling, then slumped over the navigation controls, his face wincing from the pain of forced thaw out.

Nobody was at the helm, because each move of the ship meant outward communication. Outward communication meant death.

We couldn't move the ship anywhere without using outward communication. The computer malware had trigger programming on us, so outward communication meant death.

Vladimir slumped over the controls and took charge.

He plunged the ship in a dive to China. Brent Spiner rushed onto the bridge, holding onto a ledge to keep from falling.

Some on earth had primitive radars that mistook our dive as a nuke or a Jesuit nukkake. The ship dove like a missile, whirling in a frenzy as Vladimir tried to avoid an onslaught of missiles hurled at us.

Brent yelled, "Vlad! There's a nuke coming our way. Can't you go a little slower? Because we can't communicate, they must think we're a nuke missile."

"No!" Vlad yelled. He swerved the ship out of the range of the nuke, just missing it. "Too slow. We die."

That swerve threw all of us across the room.

Each move of the ship sent out signals—outward communications. Outward communications triggered the computers over our bodies to kill or incapacitate us.

Another nuke whizzed by us.

All of us flew from one side of the ship to another. I put my hand out to give myself some cushion when my body flung itself against the wall.

"Another nuke." Vladimir snarled. "Damn."

He whirled the ship out of its way, and we all heard another missile whiz by us.

Anybody not tied down, got whirled from one end of the room to another. I got on my knees and prayed, while my balloon penis squeaked like a mouse chased by a rabid cat.

"Shut up, would you!" I snarled to myself. "How can these guys work with all this noise?"

I so wanted to give Vladimir some support, but that damn penis of mine could only screech, right in the middle of a nuclear attack.

God, what kind of a man was I? My manhood was tied up in a penis that squeaked with terror at the slightest move. Nothing I did tamed the coward. I felt like a half-breed wailing infant and Tiny Tim.

As the ship dove down to China, my penis squeaked in spasms. I felt like a woman having a panic attack.

The ship landed with a thud, and my penis shrieked so loud, it made the walls vibrate with terror. I became nauseated from embarrassment. That damn balloon penis shrieked like goblins in hysterics.

Vladimir held onto the bridge to balance himself and he went white, his skin now clammy. Oh God, we didn't need a dead Vladimir. He closed his eyes, heaved in a huge breath and slugged his body, tripping and falling, to the infirmary.

He crashed into bed and conked out.

My penis squealed and Brent had to speak over it. But he graciously ignored it. "What we just witnessed with Vladimir, was a miracle. It's amazing that guy isn't dead."

I felt bile going up my esophagus, my body heaving with shame. My heaving triggered another squeaking episode. That balloon between my legs sounded like wailing puppies. I swallowed my vomit, infuriated into turmoil and disgust. Tears of shame welled up in my eyes.

Because Hu Jintao was on Gail's marriage list, we decided to land in China for help. So all the men, myself included, got rushed into Chinese hospitals. I felt my heart lift, because I felt I would be released from my cowardly captor.

We readily agreed to general anesthesia, so the Chinese doctors could operate and fix our penises.

"I know we can replace our computers quickly here in China, and have all of our men treated promptly," Brent said. "This computer onslaught here at Church of Gail is simply too much for us to handle. So that's why we're here. I don't want to risk losing any of our men."

"Hey Brent," I said. "Isn't it kind of dangerous to be on land with a defunct computer system on Church of Gail?"

"Yes, it is," he said. "But what can we do? We're just sitting ducks here, waiting for a disaster to happen. At least now we can work on our computers. And we have the Chinese doctors to fix our penises."

I crashed my head between my hands. "Oh God, what a nightmare."

We got first class treatment. The Chinese doctors hooked us all up to IVs, and we conked out for days.

Several days later, the anesthesia wore off and I was eager to see my real penis restored. But when I unzipped my pants and saw two band-aids that criss crossed each other, I had no penis at all!

The Chinese doctors amputated my penis!

We all awakened at about the same time and none of us, with the exception of Matthew McConaughey, had a penis. All of us had a criss cross of band aids where our penises had been.

Brent stood up in bed nearby, and yelled at the nurse. "What happened to our penises?"

The nurse quickly made our beds, as if we cared about that and ignored us.

"Hey nurse, I asked you a question," Brent repeated.

The nurse bowed to us, her short, cropped hair flew down like a mop. She giggled. She raised her head and smiled, and her black hair flopped back into place. "White men's penis very valuable on black market."

"What?" Vladimir seemed completely healed from his bladder explosion.

The nurse giggled again. "Chinese doctors did not mean to steal your penises, but when they see how long and beautiful your penises. They jealous. So stole them."

"Stole them?" Brent guffawed in disgust. "They have no right to do that!"

She bowed and walked backwards.

Our angry faces glared at her.

"Soup made from white man's penis is ancient medicine for virility." She giggled.

I lifted the criss cross band aids and in place of my penis was a mangina, or a small hollow that resembled a vagina. I wondered if I now had eggs instead of sperm.

Brent and Vladimir jerked their IVs out of their arms and the rest of us followed suit.

"We go find those assholes." Vlad tromped out of the room.

We all marched like steam engines out the door, determined to find those Jesuit doctors.

After wandering past several empty surgical rooms, we found them. They were finalizing a procedure to attach our penises to themselves. It was a surgical room.

Their faces beamed with excitement.

"Stop!" Brent yelled. "Those penises don't belong to you."

We saw several small penises, freshly amputated, about two inches long lying on another table.

The Jesuit Chinese doctors laughed. "When we have your big white penises, we finally feel sex." Their chief spokesman broke into a big smile. "We bang all sorts of women."

Vladimir charged on them with judo chops, taking out several doctors. The rest he injured, so that we could pin them to the floor, and some of the others we grabbed from behind and pinned their hands and feet so they couldn't move.

I managed to pry some surgical tools from one of the doctors and handed them to the most talented physician in our group- Brent. Brent pried the rest of the surgical tools from the hands of those Chinese thieves.

Matthew McConaughey unzipped his pants. "Hey, you guys. My penis has been fully restored. They didn't mess with me."

They, apparently, didn't want Matthew's penis, which was not as fat or long as ours.

Brent had the Chinese doctors explain to him the procedures involved to restore the penises to all the men. "You tell us how to do this, so we can fix our penises."

Vladimir tightened his grip on all the doctors. "I have black belt in judo, and I finish you, if you not tell how to fix penis trouble."

Those Chinese doctors explained how they did their sex change operation for Matthew who had a vagina. Brent found it fascinating.

"Those Chinese doctors were corrupt, evil Jesuits, but they

were damn good," Brent told us later. "They were so jealous of our superior penises, they made sure to rebuild them properly."

After learning how to do a sex change operation, it was a piece of cake for Brent to surgically reattach our penises to our manginas (the male version of a vagina).

When it was my turn to be fixed, I was elated. My balloon penis was gone!

Now we just needed to fix the malware at Church of Gail, so we could be sure we wouldn't have to endure a repeat of penis terror.

We returned to Church of Gail. It was grounded for computer repairs in China. They were still trying to do a System Restore, but we were up against a wall. A System Restore did nothing.

We discovered that if we tried to contact Gail, the malware in the Church of Gail computer system might infect her computer and give her a penis. We decided that if Gail developed a penis, we would still love her. We'd just have to make love to her brain to brain, because she wouldn't have a vagina. But she hadn't gotten a penis yet, so to protect her from our malware, we refused to communicate with her until we fixed our computers.

Her sister, Sandra, in Church of Gail prison grew a penis with semen during the ordeal and raped several women in Church of Gail prison.

I knew one thing for sure, if I ever got out of this alive and with my real penis, I'd make love to Gail.

I kept this to myself, because I didn't want anybody to stop me. The only thing I regretted about the penis ordeal is that I never made love to Gail.

The Jesuits would try to kill me for going after Gail, but for me death was better than to die without having made love to Gail.

I had a heart to heart talk with Brent and told him, "I'd rather die on my feet, than live on my knees."

Brent seemed to understand. But he had no idea that I had plans to get Gail before him.

Being on Gail's marriage list meant that each day I could be a dead man.

I hated Susan Schneider from the first day Jesuits pounced

her on me. It seemed none of us would get Gail unless we seized the day.

After several weeks with a squeaking balloon penis, I felt totally emasculated.

I was living on my knees.

To go after Gail, and try to marry her, when an entire empire threatened my death for this, would put me on my feet.

No longer would the world view me as Tiny Tim. Yes, I was a man! Perhaps I would die in the attempt, but at least in my heart I'd be a man.

If I succeeded, the Jesuit lies about Gail would end, and I'd be a hero.

The physical crisis had ended, but my manliness still needed resurrection. I must do something daring, like Vladimir did to rescue us all.

I planned to announce in a mainstream broadcast, like FOX News, that I would marry Gail. After all, hadn't we already allowed Gail to make all the major broadcasts when she took over the U.S. as Empress?

Sure, the Jesuits removed this from everybody's memories, but it really happened.

My bravado would put the Jesuit Order on their knees.

Dreams of Gail consumed me. "Carpe Diem!"

The thought of marrying Gail and taking her to bed, lifted the weight from my heart.

Of course, the men would oppose me, saying it's far too dangerous. So as soon as I could safely leave Church of Gail, I'd carry out my plans in secret.

It seemed the brain reads on me were turned off. Ranked low on Gail's list of men, I perceived Jesuits did not expect me to go for Gail. This gave me an advantage over Brent.

I saw only two options before me.

One, marry Gail and respect myself as a man.

Or, two, cowardly retreat before the Jesuits, and awaken each morning with a heart of lead, filled with doubts about my honor and manhood.

Everybody who was anybody in Hollywood knew I was on Gail's marriage list. Would those Jesuits kill me just because I claimed Gail as my wife?

"No more would Jesuits rule over my heart and my penis."

I felt a bit bad for Brent, but he'd had his chances and still hadn't gotten Gail. Perhaps, I could succeed, where he failed, and then offer him marriage to Gail in place of me, if he so desired.

It wasn't that I envied Brent, but I didn't think that guy would ever take the plunge.

I no longer desired to pull the sheets over my head in shame when I awakened. No more did I want to face the day as a Benedict Arnold. Thoughts of my plan brought life to my heart.

But I'd have to leave the safety of Church of Gail to carry this out, because if Brent or Vlad heard of this, I could hear them. "No, Robin. This is far too dangerous. We don't want to lose you."

If I wanted to claim Gail, I'd have to do it alone and isolated from these men I learned to trust and love.

But after the holocaust of the past months, death seemed more certain to me than life.

"Carpe diem!"

Carpe Diem

The entire month of July 2014 I schemed how I could be with Gail. After almost losing my life and my penis for her, I now realized that nothing mattered but to be with her, to hold her in my arms and nourish her with my love.

The malware still ruled over Church of Gail and we could not see Gail's face, hear her voice or listen to her thoughts in her videos at YouTube or her emails to us.

The other guys on the marriage list struggled as I did over dying and what it meant.

But I was already dead.

I don't know what kept the other guys going. Perhaps, they still believed Gail existed somewhere out there.

It seemed Gail vanished, and my heart crashed. Each day, I wondered, would I be alive the next? Would my manhood be torn from me? Would happiness — the presence of Gail — vanish?

Jesuits severed my jugular, and I died.

I longed to see her face, taste her mouth, feel her skin.

The android dummy that Jesus gave us in place of Gail, malfunctioned, like my penis, taunting my dreams.

My clone wife Susan possessed my house, like a skeleton dragging its chains.

The night loomed over the sun. Skeletons dragged their chains, mocking my existence.

Tears flooded my pillow at night. I stared for hours at the roof, and counted the minutes of my heart. Echoes of loneliness taunted dreams. I knocked and heard echoes, longings whispered, yearnings sighed, and dreams became mist.

My dreams of Gail moaned through the night.

Beside me, tramped a wife of icicles dripping off my heart, a heart that had become a dungeon of duties and death.

Illusions and fantasies whirled about me. I floated with Gail into another realm, and Susan Schneider lost me forever.

My press performances rattled with facades. Happiness and laughter covered skeletons of darkness. Susan's chains strangled my neck and suffocated my dreams.

I faced death each day, for skeletons.

My duties, no longer confined to illusion, rose and killed my dreams, that glimmer of light that held me.

But I needed dreams to live, so that I could feel.

My heart lost itself in dreams, so that I could feel the sunrise and sunset.

Each night I cried myself to sleep, reaching out for Gail, feeling the pillow for her, staring at the ceiling through tears.

While I paraded with Susan Schneider in the façade that ruled my life, reality for me was heaven with Gail, with my body and hers fused into every breath and step of my existence.

Dreams of Gail fueled each minute of my day, while I worked on the sets for movies, while I lay my head on the pillow for sleep, into dreamland I rambled.

Between my legs, a criss cross of band-aids patched a mortal wound — the death of my dreams for manliness.

That wound raged with blood, it cascaded to hell.

I lost my soul.

My performance as the celebrity husband of Susan Schneider suffocated heaven.

Gail became a mirage.

I couldn't feel or see her. I wanted to feel her skin, smell her breath, sense her thoughts and merge our souls. This church spaceship that I lived on with my dreams, vanished into the mist.

FOX News, CNN and MSNBC — the charade- moved me like a pawn. I had the heart of a king, and yearned for my queen.

The Jesuit knight and his pawns claimed the throne.

Pyrite reigned, and glitter ruled over gold.

I cried myself to sleep every night, dreaming of heaven.

The other men on Gail's marriage list could still feel her or hold her in their dreams. For them, Gail was still real, somewhere out there in that land of make believe, where she wandered.

But, for me, she vanished, and I plunged into darkness.

Was Gail real?

Could she fill those depths in me that only heaven could fill?

Without her, my mansion became a crypt. I wandered by my star on the Hollywood Walk of Fame, and saw it vanish into the night.

Devils danced in the streets, ghouls whispered and mocked the day, the hollows of my heart echoed loneliness. The parade of life wearied me, my heart gasped for breath. Vanity of vanities, all was vanity.

I made plans, and a list.

I could feel the paper in my hands. I could feel the pen I used to write down my dreams.

1) Get your mother's wedding ring from the Tiburon mansion and custom design it into a two billion dollar wedding ring.

2) Buy a bouquet of the rarest orchids.

3) Make arrangements to have a disguise, to walk the streets of earth without paparazzi.

4) Buy the airplane ticket to Melbourne, Florida, where Gail lives.

5) Make a list of hotels to sleep in, a different one each night, to evade captors.

6) Use your iPad to research hotels, florists, ring designers.

7) Destroy the iPad after the research, and don't leave a clue to the Jesuits or anyone about what you're up to.

8) Arrange a contact at FOX News to let them read your marriage proposal to the world.

9) Get a limousine ready to drive to Gail's apartment and stand at her door.

I spaced out my moves through the month of July, planning and research first, then a blitzkrieg of action toward the end, before suspicion could be awakened, before the knight could block me from my queen.

While the men at Church of Gail struggled with malware, I struggled to come alive.

My Mother's Ring

I was close to my mother. When I went through my divorce with two women who devastated my heart, thoughts of my mother brought a balm to the frigid air I breathed in my cold marriages.

I admired Gail who stayed with her frigid husband for fifteen years and remained physically faithful to him throughout her marriage, even when Brent propositioned her in 1991. She stuck with that cold rat until 2001, just for Jesus.

If my former wives were in Gail's shoes, they would have jumped into bed with Brent at their first opportunity, not out of love, but for an opportunity to get his money.

Laughter and sunshine were the air my mother breathed. Her smile over my life was like a beam of pride over all my accomplishments. When mom and I met Prince Charles, she congratulated him for being such a good host to the true star — me. What a kick she was. But she was real, and her love for me was real, too.

When I lost her in 2001, I lost a part of my soul. It made it harder for me to stay with wife number two. With mom gone, I could no longer lie to myself and say the woman in my house loved me like mom.

Yeah, they say a man will never find a woman who loves him like his mother, and I guess it's true. But when I found Gail, or I got put on her list, I think I found a wife who could love me as much as mom did. Yeah, I knew Gail wasn't dreaming about me every day, because Brent was her man. But, if anything happened to Brent, I figured I had a chance for happiness in love.

I did some dumb things as a star. I didn't marry for fame. I married for love and naively assumed that just 'cause I was famous, I was so adorable that women would love me, too.

I decided to have an affair with my nanny because I knew my wife could care less that I left her for a nanny, 'cause now she'd get all my money.

She got millions, and my nanny became wife number two. Oh, was I dumb in those days. I should have known that if you're rich and famous, you can never get a woman to marry you for love, unless she's a saint like the virgin Mary.

Well, I wasn't exactly famous when I married my first wife, but I got famous when she had me, and my fame certainly wasn't a liability to her when divorce time came round. She fell out of love with me fast, and found a new love, my pocketbook.

I was starved in the bedroom. I mean making love to her was about as exciting as kissing the wall. This is what Gail went through with her first husband.

How I admired Gail for turning down Brent Spiner, who would die for her, to remain with her cold husband, all for Jesus.

All my wives were Mr. Hyde rude at home and Dr. Jekyll polite in public.

Like Loree McBride with Brent Spiner and Camila Alves with Matthew McConaughey, their obsession was not my happiness, but their reputation. They obsessed over public opinion, because if you're truly an inferior person, all you have is your reputation. Once you lose that, you lose all that money you stole from the person you married and slandered in court to get all their money.

Perhaps if I wasn't so starved for love, I wouldn't have had an affair with my nanny. The nanny was pregnant with my child when I married her, making her wife number two. But, alas, wife number two was no better than wife number one.

I stayed with wife number two longer, because I was in denial that I failed again to marry a woman who truly loved me. But after my mother died, and I no longer had a female companion who understood me, I felt the loneliness of my cold marriage like a crypt. The wide spaces inside my mansions echoed loneliness and desertion.

Eventually, I decided the charade was up and divorced wife

number two in 2008. It took a while to divorce this one, because I knew she was only after my money and that divorcing her could bankrupt me. But I couldn't breathe in that marriage, and the walls of my life smelled like mold.

I, and about all of Hollywood knew about the Nobel Prize winning writer that Matthew McConaughey fell in love with in 2005, while he played the lead character in the film based on her writings.

Heck, any woman who gets a movie made from her book by Steven Spielberg is gonna be known around Hollywood.

Gail didn't think she deserved any Nobel Prize, and Zack Knight, the creep Jesuit leader, made sure she never got it. But all of us in Hollywood knew the truth.

What amazed me about Gail was her willingness to allow a list of men to be put in waiting for her.

She fell in love with Brent Spiner first, and Zack Knight sabotaged that. Then she tried for a President, Vladimir Putin, and Zack Knight messed that up.

Jesuits almost murdered her. They tried poison. They tried to burn her house down. Yet, despite all that Jesuits threw at her, she never, ever betrayed her men, even if the whole world abandoned her as insane. Once she figured out that Jesuits extorted our "wives" onto us, she abandoned everything to stand by us, even willing to die for us. She had near misses on the road with mack trucks, and in 1999 and 2000 almost everything she bought that she had to ingest, Jesuits contaminated with viruses and germs, even getting her prescription drugs.

I, along with about forty other men, decided this woman was the sexiest, bravest and most beautiful Esther we'd ever come across. She looked twenty years younger than her age, with no plastic surgery and had a soul as vast as the sea, and a heart as high as the heavens.

Jesuits gave her a rare yeast infection, that would have killed her, but Brent became a doctor for Gail and advised her brain to brain how to stay alive and she survived.

That Jesuit germ took some of her looks, made her thin as a rail, and she suffered mineral loss in her teeth, but, oh, to me, she never lost her vastness or her beauty.

I understood why Brent Spiner, Vladimir Putin and Matthew

McConaughey were smitten.

After my 2008 divorce, I decided if I ever married, I would marry a woman like Gail.

Have you ever watched a movie and fallen in love with the star? You tell yourself how silly this is, that the star is just an actor and you're just a fan.

Ah yes, I was star struck. Imagine me, a star — star struck.

But I was.

Then you get to know the star, and learn that this star is for real, and has a soul like Jesus Christ and beauty like an emerald.

Well, us rich and famous guys, who observed Gail, felt Gail was this star.

Imagine how thrilled you'd be, if this star was single and willing to have a list of men who'd be put in waiting as possible husbands? Though deprived of her wealth and fame, she was actually a royal with the genes of King David and Catherine the Great.

Sounds like a fairy tale, but this was real.

So, after my divorce and a heart smashed and stomped on, I decided I would reserve my heart only for Princess Aurora.

Gail was Princess Aurora — a real Princess. She really had the genes of King David and Catherine the Great.

We did brain reads on her, and found her to have some of the deepest, truest feelings that a human being can have for another human being. Her favorite pastime was to nurture every ripple of manliness that caressed her dreams.

When she dreamed about Brent or Vladimir or Matthew, her heart flowed into their muscles, their brilliance, their depth, their manliness, their dreams and their soul.

Bright lights, fame, riches and glamour had no allure for her. She dreamed about loving her men with all her heart and soul, basking in their vastness, nurturing their greatness.

Our brain reads determined her ex-husband had only married her to get military wife pay, and tricked her into believing he had some love for her, only so he could maintain his control over her, just like my wives did to me.

After she divorced the cold skunk to go to Brent, Jesuits bankrupted her and crashed airplanes on September 11, 2001 to keep Brent from her.

The thought that a woman could love my soul, and dream about loving me all day, made me soar.

But with every fairy tale, there's a hitch.

To gain Princess Aurora, you must fight the dragon. The prince could not have his princess, unless he battled Maleficent.

We found a real Princess, but needed to battle a real dragon. We decided to fight for her to the death.

I jumped at the opportunity to be on her list, because she allowed the world to read her heart and soul through our mind-reading scans. This woman was the real deal. For me, as a Hollywood star, fortune hunters roamed the earth.

Zack Knight wasted no time to capture me and keep me from my Princess.

Within months, the press lies started. Jesuits deluged the Internet and the tabloids with lies that I loved their agent Susan Schneider.

The Jesuit Order married me to Susan Schneider.

I sighed to myself. I supposed I'd end up like Brent with Loree, Vladimir with Lyudmila and Matthew with Camila. Even the names rhymed. You'd think the public would get it.

I told myself, "I'll never let a woman trample my heart again. They're all fortune hunters."

What upset me was that once they got all my money, not only did they not miss me, but divorce thrilled them, because now they could get all my money. It made me feel like I had warts or something.

I'm the "still water, run deep" type and told myself, "You're heart's never going to the pigs again!"

But heck, even a star needs love. I'd had it with fakes who played the game of celebrity wife. I wanted a woman who had stars, rather than dollar bills, in her eyes for me.

When the woman of my dreams showed up, even though I'd be put on a list, I said, "Sign me up."

Even at fifty-six, Gail shimmered over my heart like an emerald, making most cute twenty-somethings seem like glitter.

This emerald would put me on a list to marry her?

I felt the shimmer of every crevice of her heart and floated into fairy tales.

She became more real than the air I breathed.

Brent adored her, wanting her to get someone who would kiss her footsteps as he did, finding camaraderie with those who, like him, valued a soul mate above everything.

We banded together to stay alive in our dreams for Gail.

Gerard Butler did psych profiles on all who wanted to be on her list.

I made it.

Like a teenager on his first date, my heart fluttered with butterflies at the thought of kissing her.

I suppose you need to give up this nonsense when you get older, because that fool's paradise of forever love doesn't exist, they say.

But what are fame, mansions, Mercedes, roaring crowds, Academy Awards, Emmys, tuxedos, and adoring fans if your heart is famished in a desert?

So in the middle of July 2014, I made up my mind that Gail would wear my mother's ring.

Though we could still not get online without danger to our penises, because the computer malware that affected out penises wasn't fixed until July twenty-seventh.

But we could use transporter technology to go to earth for emergencies.

I used the excuse that I was working on the sequel to *Mrs. Doubtfire* and needed to get to earth to make arrangements with the screenwriter and get the thing going.

I snuck into my Tiburon, California mansion when Susan wasn't there and snitched into my bedroom, leaping over to the safe where I kept my mother's wedding band. I also grabbed a couple of wigs, moustaches and other disguises I could use as I travelled.

It felt so good to be off that Church of Gail, which now had a computer system that tormented us. We were all very vulnerable with our Church of Gail computers down and I risked my life to be on earth, because Church of Gail was really the only safe haven for those of us on Gail's list.

I jumped into my rented car, a 2005 Toyota Corolla, and headed down the Pacific Coast, with the ring in my car. I chose a car that looked like it belonged to someone with an income of around twenty-five thousand a year.

As I stared out at the vista of the ocean, I felt like I was flying to be with Gail. I plopped in my CD of Keith Jarrett playing a jazz tune of *Somewhere over the Rainbow*, and hummed it to myself. The piano plucked its flutters of joy over the vast shore before me. The shore stretched for miles, rocks jutted up like fortresses in the beach and sea. I chose this route to dream of Gail, who made me feel free and vast. The sun glared on the horizon over the shimmering sea. I flowed into the music with dreams of Gail and calm came over me, soothing the war in my heart.

Another track started, with high notes lingering on the piano. . .*When I Fall in Love.* I then played the same tune from Brent Spiner's *Ol' Yellow Eyes Is Back.*

It seemed nobody knew I was driving this car.

I actually created a masked credit card with a fake name and used that for all my purchases. This particular card let me create a new credit card and number that only worked for one transaction at a time.

It seemed I would land in Los Angeles without being noticed. With that long drive, I tested the Jesuits to see if they were reading my mind.

You see, they threatened to kill any man on Gail's marriage list who made a move towards her.

If I could pull off that haul down the Pacific Coast Highway to L.A. with my mother's wedding band in the car, then my dream to land on Gail's doorstep seemed within my grasp.

The sun shimmered through layers of streaks, iridescent on the horizon. My manhood soared.

My heart lapped on the shore. I closed my eyes and soaked in a fading sun, while a breeze passed over my heart.

Surely the Jesuits would plunge my car over the cliff to the rocks below, if they could read my mind now.

Almost in L.A. and still alive, I was elated. "You Jesuit bastards you, looks like I pulled one over on you."

I would really hold Gail in my arms. My soul flew over the shore and up to the sky.

In Brentwood, California now, I headed over to my favorite custom design jewelry store in this suburb near Santa Monica. It was in a strip mall.

I greeted the jewelers, who had lived at Church of Gail at one time. I knew I could trust these jewelers not to hand me over to the Jesuits or betray me. They were good people.

With a blonde wig and moustache, and contacts to make my eyes dark brown rather than blue, no one recognized me, except my jeweler friend, who knew me too well not to recognize me.

"It's so good to see you!" the lady jeweler said. "How're you doing?"

I pulled out my mother's ring. "I want you to redesign my mother's ring and don't tell a soul you did this."

Next, I flapped onto her counter, a picture of a ring with two carat emeralds, one on each side, and two carat diamonds, one on each side of a four carat diamond, all on a delicate, white gold band.

Each jewel was round and shimmered in the light. This design and coloring would make my Gail, a winter in coloring, glow with my love for her. The braided, delicate ring suited Gail's soft natural clothing personality.

I'd bought David Kibbe's *Metamorphoses* a long time ago, and memorized the soft natural section, so that anything I bought for Gail would flatter her. I also memorized Carole Jackson's *Color Me Beautiful* to make sure the ring's diamonds and emerald had the cool, crisp winter coloring.

The more valuable emeralds had a green so deep and transparent they shimmered blue when light hit them. This suited my Gail, whose heart shimmered like an emerald.

"How lovely. Who's the special lady?"

"I can't say," I smiled. "But this needs to be a surprise."

"I understand." The jeweler seemed confused. "But don't you need to get divorced first?"

"Under Gail's Conspiracy Law, marriages to Jesuit clone wives are invalid, so I'm not married to Susan. But the press always makes Susan my wife." I stroked my chin. "I want this ring to be worth around two billion dollars."

The jeweler's mouth opened wide in shock. "It's just a wedding ring, right?"

"Oh, but this lady is special. She's worth two billion dollars." I smiled in anticipation. "Besides, I've never met her yet."

"What!"

"Yeah, I want to wow her over and make sure she says 'yes.'"

The jeweler smiled and wagged her finger at me. "You sneaky devil you, when do you want it? I won't tell a soul."

"As soon as possible. I have to get back to Church of Gail. I plan on sleeping with it in my pillow."

"I just happen to have a rare diamond worth about a million dollars. One of my celebrity clients turned in their ring after a divorce to get some cash." The jeweler went to the back to show me the diamond. It shimmered in brilliance like heavenly Jerusalem descending.

"Wow!" I held the stone up. "This four carat beauty will surely win over the heart of that fair maiden."

"I also have two emeralds with a blue shimmer, very valuable, highest quality."

I paid for it with my masked credit card. Once I used the card I ripped it up, since this card was designed to be used only one transaction per card, then the number changed for the next card. The card was also designed to work without my signature, so it left no evidence that Robin Williams bought emeralds and diamonds to transform his mother's ring into a two billion dollar dazzler.

Once I got the ring, I held it up and said, "What a beauty, just like the woman who'll wear it."

I drove my Toyota back to the car rental, and turned it in. From there I contacted Vladimir Putin at Church of Gail. He used Star Trek-like transporter technology to transport me back to Church of Gail with all my belongings, my costumes, and my mother's redone wedding ring.

I kept checking my penis to be sure it had not turned into a balloon.

Back in my quarters at Church of Gail, I placed that ring on a table. Every day, I gazed at it admiring its shimmers as I waited at Church of Gail for the day I'd marry Gail.

If any of the guys came into my quarters, and asked about the ring, I said, "Just admiring this beauty. It's my mother's ring and will be Gail's if I end up marrying her. It helps me deal with the balloon penis. Suffering a bit of Post Traumatic Stress." The stuff about the Post Traumatic Stress was true, but nobody knew that the way I'd deal with it, was to marry Gail within a month. That was far too daring and dangerous, so no one guessed my plans.

I slept with it inside of my pillow. When I awakened the next day I stared at it all day, and placed it next to the Gail dummy Jesus gave me to make love to in place of Gail.

So while the Jesuits tried to kill me with their malware at Church of Gail, I stared at that ring and floated to the moon.

At Church of Gail we could choose which view we wanted from our windows, to give us the illusion we didn't live on a spaceship.

For my view, I basked in a panorama along the Pacific coast of the sun setting in a cirrostratus sky over an emerald sea shimmering sapphire sparkles.

I tucked the emerald and diamond ring inside my pillow, lay my head down and lost myself into the vastness of Gail.

Dreams of Paradise

After a month and a half without her voice or the sight of her, I finally saw Gail on July twenty-seventh on one of her YouTube videos.

Breath taken with her majesty, I stood aghast. I could feel her in my dreams. I could clutch her to my heart. I would never lose her again.

She surrendered everything: reputation, fame, wealth and family for me, her king.

Did such a woman exist? It was I who surrendered all for my lovers, driven by a need to prove myself worthy of love. From my childhood onwards, I always had my dad on my shoulder. As a child, everything I did was wrong, and it didn't matter if it was true or not that I was bad and should have done better.

Because I had to believe it was my fault that my dad frowned over all I did; because, though I'd never admit it, he was a bit unfair to me. But I knew he'd never change, and knowing he'd never change horrified me with the hopelessness of the universe.

You see, by blaming myself for my dad's flaws, it kept me in control of my universe, because I could control what I did, but couldn't control what dad did.

So I kept telling myself, "You just need to be more patient, or smart, or reliable. Once you change, everything will be alright."

But deep down, I knew if I changed, it would not be alright.

I'd still be a failure to my dad.

To face the fact that my dad's approval had nothing to do with me, made me feel out of control, like it was my job to maintain the earth in its orbit and if I failed, the earth would die.

I needed to feel that I had some control over my destiny, so I lied to myself and told myself that I could somehow please my dad.

When it dawned on me that his behavior had very little to do with me, it made me rebel against him in everything to prove to myself that he didn't matter. Therefore, I told myself that nothing he said was right.

But some of what he taught me was correct. It made me realize that he expected perfection, which I couldn't give him. Admitting he was right about some things meant I couldn't write him off.

He'd always be my dad. I couldn't keep him from being my dad any more than I could stop breathing to remain alive.

But I could never make him happy no matter what I did. My mere existence was an abomination to him.

Knowing that I had no control over my dad's approval, made me feel that I could never be good enough unless I attained perfection.

Rather than admit that perfection for me was impossible on this present earth, I chose rather to accept some blame for my dad's disapproval of me. This made me believe that I had the power to transform a cold father who would never change.

It overwhelmed me to admit that my dad's anger was unfair just because I couldn't be perfect, according to his definition of perfection, which was always changing. To admit that my dad had impossible expectations, meant I'd have to admit that sometimes you can be in a relationship with a person who won't change and that the situation is hopeless, that the person is cruel and nothing will change that.

Such a bleak conclusion I couldn't handle, so I just lied to myself.

If my dad could never become a positive and encouraging person, it meant the universe was filled with cruel people who could not change.

This darkness clouded my soul and put me into despair. So I needed to believe my dad could change, so I could see some light at the end of the tunnel.

I never overcame the script he shoved into my subconscious that if only I was good enough, I could have approval and love.

I was on an unending treadmill, because for people like my

dad, once I did something right, I did five things wrong.

It crushed me too much to believe that my father could be so unfair. Because there was nothing I could do to change it.

So I told myself these icebergs of rigidity in my life would change if only I was better and if only I had the virtues needed to make them happy.

Far more palatable to blame myself for my shortcomings, than admit some in my family had ice hearts set forever into rigidity.

Surely I deserved the shame my dad heaped on me. Surely he would not hate me just for being alive.

It horrified me to admit I had a father, who would always remain as frigid as an iceberg.

This started a cycle with me, where I married women like my father, driven by the need to get my dad's approval.

I'd buy mansions, showering my wives with love, attention and riches to earn approval from them, apologizing for letting them down.

But even when I apologized, they still complained, still nagged, still frowned over who I was, what I dreamed about, and what I cared about.

I was just a failure, who could never get it right, no matter if I showered them with attention, gifts, riches, time and affection.

Didn't women need love? But they'd scream at me, "You're not listening to me! Why'd you buy all those horses. We really need another guest bedroom for my family."

"I'm sorry. I didn't know that we need twenty guest rooms."

"Well, you're famous and we can't insult our guests by expecting them to stay in a motel. Where's your pride?"

So I bought the guest room, and then it was something else I did wrong.

Finally, I came to the conclusion that once a woman tasted my riches, she became obsessed with it, that my riches ruined all my women.

They tailed me, screaming at me — never happy. It was always my fault. I was hopeless. I was an idiot. I was a bastard.

With each wife, I could hear her screeching at me with rage so loud, the walls echoed temper tantrums and books flew across the room.

I'd give in and have peace for a while.

But nothing worked. They loved the control they had over my bank account.

Finally, I'd had it. I knew wife number two would sue me till she bled me dry, but those vast rooms, and chandeliers, and the damask tablecloths, wineries, orchards, thirty-two acre yards, and fancy china only bounced from books thrown across the room, or rages of fire in my soul from broken windows because of a baseball bat hurled at me. My existence was a war zone.

If I disobeyed a command, the wife would go into hysterics.

This time I refused their demands. I was tired of walking on a tightrope.

Wife number two filed for divorce.

To admit they only loved my money meant I was living with my father again. Only this time he reincarnated himself into my wife.

After two divorces, and billions splurged pacifying icebergs of disapproval, who'd never thaw no matter what I did, I realized I was surrounded by a darkness that no light could conquer.

I'd dropped into a dungeon without food or water. A wall of China stood between my heart and love.

The very wealth I used to buy approval and love became my curse.

So when Zack Knight gave me a balloon penis, it just reinforced the hopelessness that I always fell short somehow.

The balloon penis was the last straw.

I saw it as my dad attached between my legs, laughing at me, along with Zack Knight.

For me, approval and true love were not to be had.

The balloon penis reinforced to me that my dad was right. I was hopeless.

Even worse, that I would be forever a failure, because I could never meet the standards my dad and wives set for me.

Imperfect people expected perfection. This was a prison from which there was no escape. Nothing I did fixed it. I plunged into the despair of a forever disapproval.

Once my wives learned I had a deep-rooted inferiority complex, rather than try to build me up and get me to accept myself as worthy, they went into a tirade or got moody and sulked.

To nurture, accept, and love me, never crossed their minds.

I gave into their demands to pacify them, only to find they wanted more. Then they made me feel more worthless. Then when I gave them what they wanted, they wanted even more, all the while screeching at me for my idiocy, making more demands.

When I finally realized that the guilt I felt was a player on a chessboard for them to manipulate, and that they were only happy when they controlled my bank account, I ingested the truth and got sick to my stomach.

The hardest blow came when I realized they could murder me for my money, and not lose any sleep over it.

Only when I lived at Church of Gail did I find those who loved and accepted me as I was.

All the tears I shed to show my shame for angering them, all the money I spent to lavish them with mansions, waterfalls, vineyards, tennis courts, Mercedes, vacations, did nothing to transform them into a person who genuinely cared about me, and would miss me at my death.

It seemed the more I lavished my wealth on a woman, the less she loved me, and the more she obsessed over my money.

Wife number two convinced me I couldn't get a woman to love me more than my money.

My heart plummeted to hell.

When I learned about Gail and realized she had turned down Brent in 1991 to stay with her poor, but cold husband to be true to God, I realized that there was *one* person on this planet who could not be bought.

Her mere existence and that she allowed a marriage list of guys to wait for her, gave me hope that I could reinstate beauty and love into my universe.

It seemed my money corrupted all my lovers, turning them from good women to cold-hearted hags.

But Catherine the Great and King David brought a beauty to my life that I never dreamed possible.

I was star struck. I flung open my coffin, and embraced the sun in Gail. I closed my eyes and basked in her warmth. I breathed in a wisp of fresh spring air. I floated with happiness. It was like all that happened to me from twenty to sixty-three never happened, and I was a young lad courting my high school sweetheart.

My woman was pure as the snow and devoted like Esther and Ruth.

I never could kill that part of me that wanted to wow my woman with the depth of my feeling for her. So I kind of fell back into my old behavior of trying to wow the woman with my riches to earn her love.

My psychiatrist Gerard told me I needed to stop this, that if a woman truly loved me, I didn't need to prove myself to her with two billion dollar rings and twenty room mansions.

But it's so deeply ingrained inside of me to be like this and I love to spoil my woman, especially a woman who won't use it against me, but would honor my undying devotion for her.

Gail once said in 2002 that she'd marry the first guy on her marriage list who showed up to consummate the marriage. "If Brent shows up, I'll marry him, because I'm only with Vladimir now, because I don't think Brent will show up. Not after 9-11."

The marriage list had gotten longer and I now planned to be the first guy to show up.

By August fourth, all of us men could go to earth and be protected under Church of Gail's computer systems. After a month and a half, they fixed the malware and it was safe for us to use the Internet.

However, I checked to see if they were reading my mind.

I saw no brain reads on me. The Church of Gail scientists weren't checking my memories or my thoughts. I presumed that no one, including the Jesuits, anticipated my plans for Gail.

To make it a total surprise, I never talked to Gail brain to brain ever.

Now safe to go online, I disguised myself as another man and ordered rare orchids from a florist with my masked credit card which I'd pick up in person on August eleventh.

I Take the Leap

The thought of Parkinson's never entered my head the last day that I lived on earth.

I knew I risked my life to marry Gail, but just couldn't take the humiliation of feeling like a failure anymore. I'd rather die on my feet than live on my knees.

Perhaps it was something deeply ingrained in me from my dad, this feeling that I never quite measured up.

When Gail came into my life, she made me feel like a hero. I adored her for that. She freed me from this feeling that I didn't measure up, so I wanted to die for her.

Gail never made us feel like anything less than heroes, even when the Jesuits bankrupted her and almost killed her. She was consumed with nourishing our manliness, because our greatness was her daily bread.

Whenever I thought of her, she completed me. She integrated those parts of me that squeaked and grated, soothed wars within, so that I moved with precision. She fused me with endurance into vast plains, so that I soared to mountaintops.

Zack Knight used my balloon penis to fling me from that mountaintop down to a valley of skeletons. I returned to the skeletons of all those feelings I'd overcome because of Gail. Zack brought me back into captivity to my torturers, so that I was back on the treadmill, trying to gain approval, this feeling that I wasn't a man and needed to measure up.

I was back on the treadmill. I'd never get off until I measured up, but I could never measure up and I stumbled and fell. But this time I didn't get up. I remained humiliated on the floor, unable to right myself, unable to get off my knees onto my feet.

I tried to think of Gail. I felt for her with my fingers, used the Gail dummy to remind myself of her.

But I remained on the treadmill. I'd stumble and fall and then get right back on it. That month and a half of silence, with a squeaking penis, devastated my peace.

I heard that squeak in my dreams. It followed me throughout the day and kept me up at night with nightmares.

Gail vanished like the morning mist.

Throughout the day I searched for her — in my dreams, in my imaginations.

She'd vanished like the morning mist. She seemed a delusion.

At night, I felt for her in my bed, but the Gail dummy only squeaked as its arms moved to remind me Gail wasn't real.

In Gail's place, I saw my dad and all my wives and Susan wagging their fingers at me, telling me to get back on the treadmill.

Every time I tried to think of Gail, my penis squeaked. After the squeaking stopped, it continued in my nightmares. Then I'd awaken and check my penis every minute to be sure it was not a balloon, to be sure I was a man.

With Gail vanquished from me, I became tormented with doubts about my manliness. Surely I lost her because I failed to be a man. I needed to get back on that treadmill to find my manliness and find Gail.

Back on the treadmill I ran and ran, but still couldn't find Gail, still couldn't find my manliness. I still felt like a balloon penis. When could I feel Gail's pride in my manliness? But I kept running and slugging on that treadmill, and I couldn't see Gail, I could only see a balloon penis.

I was tormented with this feeling that I would be a balloon penis forever. That I had become that balloon and could not be anything else.

I tried to shove Gail into my thoughts, to feel like a man. But my nightmares of a squeaking penis still seemed more real than Gail.

I needed a Gail I could feel, taste, or touch, not an illusion or a video image.

Once Gail vanished into the mist, I fell apart. It made it worse that I could not see or hear her videos for over a month.

After we fixed the malware at Church of Gail, I still had nightmares of my dad and all my wives wagging their fingers at me in disapproval, and it was as if Gail had never come into my life.

Gail seemed like a distant dream and so the peace I got from her vanished, and again, I was tormented with doubt about my manhood.

Even though my penis had returned, I still felt like a guy with a balloon penis.

I was trapped on this treadmill. To get off, I had to marry Gail and kiss her lips, feel her skin and hold her in my arms. To do this, I'd need to be a hero, because Jesuits threatened death to any man on Gail's marriage list who went for her.

I knew what I had to do, so that I could be a man again.

Thus far, it seemed my plan went forward without a hitch.

My disguises worked, and no one seemed to recognize me. I used a different credit card number for all my transactions. I used a fake name and identification for all my transactions, and looked like a blonde guy with brown eyes everywhere I went. I even dressed Michael Jackson style, to stray away from my usual persona. It looked kind of silly on me, but I was more concerned about disguising myself than respectability right now.

I stayed at a different hotel every night. I carried my iPad with me everywhere.

I had composed a marriage proposal and printed it and placed it in my luggage. I would read it when I gave Gail her flowers.

Oh, I felt so brave. I felt so manly.

Thus far, my risk was high but not formidable. I'd taken chances, but hadn't crossed the line yet. So, I figured.

I slept with that wedding ring inside my pillow case every night. I cuddled it in my dreams.

I waited until the last day, to make my final move. This was the tricky one. This was where I might get caught.

It would have been great if I could have done this with the cooperation of the guys at Church of Gail, but alas, they'd never approve of my mission. Too risky.

How was I to fly from California to Melbourne, Florida without the Jesuits finding out? I was certain they did genetic scans on all people who flew into Florida to ensure that no guy on Gail's marriage list would dare take that final plunge. Too bad I couldn't use Vladimir's supersonic jet. I could fly from California to Florida in minutes in that thing.

Yeah, but that's what Jesuits would expect a guy from Gail's marriage list to do.

The Jesuits wouldn't expect a guy to use a regular, commercial airliner. Or so I hoped.

Well, thus far, my disguise seemed to work. I decided I'd fly under a fake name. But I wanted first class, so I could be sure to get a seat by myself, lest someone on the jet would recognize me. I'd use my acting skills to transform my voice into another character other than myself, which is what I'd been doing all along any ways this week.

Using the phone for this was too risky. Voice prints would give me away. I'd been making all my reservations online, using my fake persona and masked credit cards from my iPad and not using a Church of Gail computer, which is what the Jesuits would expect.

The men at Church of Gail and the Jesuits apparently had no idea I was planning this, so they weren't using scanners to find my genetic profile. If I did anything to make the Jesuits suspicious, they'd start scanning for my profile, then I'd be finished.

Because I was doing this on my own and had to keep it a big secret, I took big chances. Normally, the guys could put a shield over themselves to try and block their genetic profile from Jesuit scanners. But since I was doing this independent of Church of Gail, my only defence from the genetic scanners was surprise.

The Jesuits simply were not expecting me to do this, so they weren't scanning for my profile.

Driving from California to Florida was out of the question. That took too long and was too obvious. Staying at various hotels in Los Angeles and California up till now worked, because they were all connected to locations for various film projects. This was how I kept Church of Gail off my back.

I also bought a cooler and shoved it with frozen T.V. dinners, sandwiches, water bottles, drinks, and plastic cutlery, so I wouldn't have to eat out and give myself away.

I made sure all hotels I stayed in had a microwave and a refrigerator. Eating out could lead to death by poisoning, so I decided to imitate Gail and never eat out while I was on this mission to be with her.

Though it was true that Gail couldn't afford to eat out, it was also harder for Jesuits to poison home cooked food.

Leaving the food in the car could be a problem, because the Jesuits could poison the food in the car, after I parked the car. So I made sure if I had food in the car, to purchase it on my last stop for the day. I usually stayed in the hotel all day and worked off my iPad so I wouldn't be recognized and so that I could watch my food. I felt safer staying in all day, less likely to be noticed and snagged.

So I went from hotel to hotel, while I researched and planned my itinerary that last week I was alive on earth. Once I checked in, I stayed in all day and didn't go out, in case Jesuits may enter my hotel room and raid my refrigerator and put drugs or germs into my food.

I tried to keep the Jesuits off my back, by donning disguises everywhere I went and using masked credit cards and never using the phone. Those voice prints got us guys in trouble before. Them damn Jesuits located us once and almost wiped us all out.

I never requested room service or asked them to call and awaken me the next morning. I avoided the phone like the plague.

Of course, the Jesuits could find me when I used the iPad by scanning the genetic profile of the originator of the online communications; but because they weren't expecting me to do this, thus far, I seemed to be moving forward without a hitch. My iPad was set up with an encrypted password and all my communications on it were encrypted.

Okay, Robin, you know when you make that reservation for the flight from L.A. to Melbourne, the Jesuits might catch you. How you gonna work around this?

I checked in at Hotel California in Santa Monica, my last hotel stop before I'd fly out of California the next day. It was right on the beach, certainly not close to the airport like the Jesuits would expect. I chose a hotel not too fancy, so I could go unnoticed until I left for the airport. I would wear my disguise until I made my announcement to marry Gail.

Well, I certainly would not make any reservations at Hotel California or with the airlines under the name Robin Williams, that's for sure!

Those Jesuits probably had the genetic scanners set up on all flights into Florida. They'd catch me for sure.

Well, Robin, you want to bail out now?

Hell, no! Carpe diem. I'm a man. I'm going to marry Gail.

Okay. You know they'll catch you. So what are you gonna do?

I'll intimidate them! I'll be so daring that they wouldn't dare try and stop me, without getting their butts exposed.

What if they crashed the plane? Well, well, boy will Gail have a story to write. It will expose them. Nasty exposure. They wouldn't like it.

What if I managed to land in Florida? They'd probably shoot me somewhere before I saw Gail. Then they'd replace me with my clone and no one would know they murdered me.

What if they shot me before I made it to the L.A. airport? Well, I'll have the wedding ring on me and it sure wouldn't make them look good to shoot me with Gail's wedding ring on me, would it? Yeah, but if they killed me before I reached the airport that wouldn't be good, better stay in my disguise until made it to the airport.

Well, Robin, you still want to land on Gail's door step? You know, you might die.

Hell, yeah. But if I died, what a way to go!

I'd take my chances. It was Gail or die. I'd rather die on my feet than live on my knees.

I'd grown out my beard that week, and was wearing fake glasses over my brown eyed contacts, to make it appear that brown eyes were my natural color.

However, I planned to shave tomorrow and look nice for to-morrow's flight. I only went around with the beard 'cause it made me look sloppy, like I wasn't planning anything like a marriage proposal.

I, all of a sudden, got a bad feeling. You know, once I buy that ticket, my goose is cooked.

I better make the announcement that I'll marry Gail at the

L.A. airport tomorrow night, or even better right before I arrive. I'll arrange a press release. I'll invite the news team to come out to Hotel California and grant me an interview.

Those Jesuits wouldn't dare crash that jet after I make the announcement to marry Gail!

I conked out and fell asleep. Too drained from all the excitement. Thus far, my plans seemed to be going forward without a hitch.

When I awakened, I wrote down what I'd say to the press in the lobby at Hotel California before I headed for the airport to marry Gail. I stuffed the note in my pocket, and worked on memorizing it. I had a bad case of nerves, so my memory wasn't as sharp as usual.

I did have a cell phone, but reserved it for emergency use. I'd use that phone to contact the news people, to invite them to come out to Hotel California for a news conference.

I thought I better make that speech before I go to the L.A. airport. The lines of the speech ran over and over in my mind.

"I'm about to take a flight to Melbourne, Florida to marry Gail Chord Schuler. She's not expecting me, but I'm on her marriage list, and I bought her a two billion dollar wedding ring, and I have this bouquet of rare orchids that I'll give her as a present."

"Mr. Williams, aren't you married to Susan Schneider?"

"No, I'm not," I'd answer.

"But wasn't there a picture of you and Susan together recently? We haven't heard of a divorce."

"That marriage was a fraud from the beginning. I've been engaged to Gail since 2010, and in love with her since 2008."

"How could you be engaged and we not know of it?"

"It's been kept secret from the mainstream news media."

"Is Gail expecting you?"

"Nope."

"You sure she'll say 'yes'?"

"Well," I would smile. I would then show the orchids, and the two billion dollar wedding ring. "You see this ring? It's worth two billion dollars."

"Who is Gail Chord Schuler?"

"She'd be a Nobel prize winning writer, except the Jesuits sabotaged that. The Jesuits oppose my marriage to her, that's why you don't know about it."

"Mr. Williams, why are you marrying this lady?"

"Because I love her enough to die for her."

"Mr. Williams, what will happen to Susan Schneider?"

"Thank you so much for talking to me," I'd say. "I must leave now and meet my future bride."

Yeah, that should cover all the bases. I imagine they'd ask me other questions, but I just won't answer them, unless I want to.

I'd dare those Jesuits to crash the jet after I announce my intentions to the world.

I drove in my rented car to a florist, and picked up the bouquet of rare orchids I'd ordered online. I did very little talking when I went out, because if Jesuits caught my voice on surveillance cameras, they might nab me.

The orchids looked like one of those bouquets that a bride holds at her wedding. It was a swoop of rare orchids that drooped with magnificence from my hand.

I returned to my private suite at Hotel California and sat on a divan in the living room section of the suite.

I swooped my hand over my iPad and my fingers trembled a bit. This would be it. After this, I'd either live or die.

It was 11 a.m. I booked a flight for that evening to arrive in Melbourne, Florida on August twelfth from L.A.

In case I had to cancel, I continued to use a masked credit card that changed its number for each transaction.

The Jesuits knew about me now.

I'd just stay inside my room and not go anywhere, until it was time to call the local FOX News station and make the announcement.

I made sure the door was locked. It had several dead bolts.

Each private suite was like a mini house, with a living room area, a bedroom, a bath, small frig, microwave, kitchen sinks, dining room area. There was a view of the beach from my window, with venetian blinds.

I paced the stone floor and prayed.

If they nabbed me in the hotel on the way out, I'd just make my announcement to marry Gail from the hotel.

Okay, now was the time to put aside all my costumes. I went to the mirror and removed the contact lenses, so that my natural blue eyes returned. I now looked like Robin Williams.

I lay back on the hotel bed and dreamed of Gail, staring up at the wooden ceiling fan. This Hotel California where I stayed in Santa Monica, was a modest hotel, with a AAA sign outside. It was the sort of hotel you'd expect a middle class person to stay in, certainly not one where Robin Williams would stay.

There were surveillance cameras in the hotel lobby. I figured I'd get caught on camera, if those Jesuits dared to nab me as I headed for the airport.

I looked at my watch. Time was around 2 p.m. August 11, 2014. I heard a knock on my door. It was probably room service. I'd just tell them that I didn't need it.

I walked in my slippers to the door, looked out the peephole.

It was the police! I decided to ignore them. I hadn't done anything wrong.

They knocked again. "Mr. Williams, we know you're in there. You're under arrest."

Under arrest? What had I done? Geez, did someone frame me for a drug deal?

I better open the door. "Let me see your badges." I went to the window. They showed their badges, they were all dressed in LAPD uniforms. One officer had a huge bag full of cocaine. Shoot, I'd been framed. It must have been Susan.

It was usually better to cooperate with the police. I opened the door to let them in.

When I opened the door, three officers jumped into my suite, slammed the door behind them and bolted it. The leader grabbed my hands and shoved them into handcuffs.

The one with the bag of cocaine, had gloves on his hands. He reached into the bag and scattered cocaine everywhere, on my bed, all over the floor. He headed to the bathroom and threw it all over the bathroom.

These officers removed their uniform shirts and underneath

they revealed t-shirts that had the IHS Jesuit symbols on their shirts.

The leader laughed. "So you think you're going to marry Gail?"

I rolled my eyes, and dashed for the front door to run away, but one of the guys stuck out his foot and I stumbled to the floor. With my hands in cuffs, I probably wouldn't get very far, but I planned to crash out the windows.

The guy who tripped me, put his foot on my back and dared me to move. He pulled out a gun and shoved it into my head.

One officer grabbed me by the shoulders and another by the feet and swung me over to the bed. I landed face down with my hands in cuffs behind my back. I tried to cut off my hands with the cuffs and escape without hands, but the officer sat me up on the bed and placed a clear bag over my head.

Then I heard another knock on the door, and the leader went to look out my peephole. "Shit," he said. "It's Tom."

"Should we let him in?" another asked.

"Yeah, we better, 'cause he might talk."

"I haven't done anything wrong," I said, my head inside the bag.

The leader opened a drawer, and got a scarf from one of my outfits and tied it around my neck. He tightened the scarf so that I could feel my breathing passages constricting.

They let Tom in and he gasped. "Why, that's Robin Williams!"

To my amazement, one of the officers put a gun to Tom's head. "Yeah, don't we know it, and you're going to report that he killed himself, or we'll make you another suicide."

It looked like my Jesuit clone wife Susan called the police and made up a story about me.

The officer in the bathroom, shut the door behind him, and was apparently still dumping cocaine all over the bathroom.

They shoved Tom into a chair and made him watch the whole thing. "What are you all doing?" Tom asked.

The leader smirked. "What do you think we're doing? Though I have to warn you if you talk too loud, this gun has a silencer on it."

The leader tossed his silencer gun to the officer who had his gun into Tom's head. The officer caught the replacement and plunged the silencer gun into Tom's head. Then he removed the gun he'd been using, and tossed it to the leader, who caught it.

Now they could kill Tom and make it look like a suicide.

Oh Jesus, I said, is there any way I can stay alive? Oh help me, Jesus! Are you mad at me because I usurped Brent Spiner, who was number one on Gail's marriage list?

Would these Jesuits murder me in cold blood right in front of this Tom, who was obviously not one of them? "Help!" I screamed.

I felt the scarf around my neck suffocate me, and I started gagging for breath.

"Hey, didn't Robin just try to talk?" Tom said. "But I didn't hear anything. Is that bag over his head some sort of silencer, so that he can scream and nobody can hear anything?"

"Shut up." The officer with the gun to Tom's head shoved it harder into his head.

It seemed that with this bag over my head, I could scream and nobody could hear me, even two feet away from me. The bag silenced my screams. I could see that only Jesus could save me now, and I prayed silently to myself. Oh Jesus, I'm sorry I didn't ask your advice before I did this. Please forgive me. But whatever happens, I don't want to do anything to help those Jesuits harm Gail. Though I'd like to live, it's more important to be a man.

The leader laughed, "He wants to die like a man!" The scarf tightened around my neck and I gagged for breath. I fought for every breath. They removed the bag and put a latex female mask over my face. The mask had holes for me to breathe and to see.

The third officer ripped off my clothes and slipped a frilly dress over my head.

"Oh, doesn't he look cute?" He taunted me.

The leader nodded his head with disapproval while viewing a scanner.

They sat me up and circled round me, all viewing the scanner.

Tom sat frozen in his chair. The officer still had the silencer gun to his head.

The leader finally spoke. "Our brain reads show that Robin is willing to die for Gail. He won't cooperate with us. He'd rather die than stay married to Susan."

The officer with the gun to Tom's head spoke next. "Well, should we let Robin live?"

The leader's eyes jumped to the scanner. "Wait, there's a message from Zack Knight." His eyes scanned the message. "Zack Knight says, 'Kill the bastard, and make it look like a suicide. He'll never cooperate with us. This was a close one. He almost had a press conference to shame us into submission. If Tom opens his mouth, kill him, too.' "

The leader looked sober and spoke to Zack Knight, who must have had a microphone installed onto the scanner. "Boss, Robin Williams does not seem like the suicide type."

"Yeah," the third officer agreed.

"Zack says it's too late to change our plans. Susan has cancelled Robin's flight to Florida. Robin's got a two billion dollar ring inside his pillow. Get it. Take the orchids out of the hotel."

The third officer shook the pillow cover off my pillow and the ring jumped out.

He held it up and whistled. "Phew, what a doozy." He smiled and laughed. "Looks like we can retire."

The orchids just disappeared. I presumed Jesuits used transporter technology to dispose of them.

The scarf was so tight around my throat, I felt like I was drowning. All around me became fuzzy, and faded out.

The bag went back over my head, but I couldn't scream, because I couldn't breathe. The leader's tight jerks of the scarf around my neck caused the latex mask to tumble down my face. As the scarf tightened around my neck, I only saw the mask in front of my eyes, blocking my view.

My lungs heaved in desperation for air. My life ebbed in and out and I fell in and out of consciousness.

I knew I would see Gail in heaven. A vision of her passed over my mind. I knew I'd be seeing Jesus soon. My muscles spasmed from lack of oxygen and a swaying sensation swirled about me. Blackness, then whiteness, and then blackness and I grew weaker till I shrank away into darkness.

All went black.

My head knocked over like concrete, with a thud. My lungs heaved for air, received none, and the breathing stopped.

I wheezed and my lungs went into a panic for air, while I felt pressure, like a boa around my neck. The neck bones crunched, and I spasmed to my death.

Thoughts of Gail floated over me.

My soul rose above my body, like a ghost on a swan. While my body below, with no pulse, spasmed.

They stuffed a dildo up the anus of my dead body, plopping the body down flat onto the bed. When they plopped me, the cocaine on the bed fluffed into the air.

That dildo they used was about the size of the one that Brent and Vladimir created for Gail in 2011.

The officer came out of the bathroom and laughed, "I put so much cocaine in that bathroom that I filled up the tub."

Tom vomited into the nearest garbage pail.

My soul floated above the scene.

They didn't know that a soul has eyes.

Jesus appeared next to me, embraced me and kissed my cheek. "Good job, Robin." He fisted me. "Carpe diem."

So my body lay on the bed, drowned in cocaine. My head wore a woman's mask inside a plastic bag, and I had a dildo stuffed up my anus.

"Zack Knight makes me so sad," Jesus said.

"Yeah, he killed me." I said.

Jesus nodded His head in agreement. "Zack Knight instructed Susan to hire those officers as hit men to murder you. Not only has he killed you, but he had Susan bribe the police department to lie and say you killed yourself by auto-erotic asphyxiation."

"Why did they put a dress on me?"

"They wanted to make it look like you enjoyed auto-erotic asphyxiation so much that you lost your head in orgasm, and accidentally killed yourself."

Jesus pulled me aside and frowned.

We watched them manipulate the penis on my dead body, so that it ejaculated all over the room.

Jesus looked depressed. "My brave Robin, already the Jesuits have flooded the news agencies with the lie that you committed suicide."

"Oh, Jesus, I was murdered!"

The Lord took me up to heaven in my young body.

A floating window opened before me, and I saw Gail writing a book about me.

Then the window faded.

Then I saw Gail, in her millennial form, with perfect beauty, gazing at the sky. A mist embraced her, and lifted her to gates that glowed like the sun.

Brent joined me, and we flowed through the gates with Gail.

Gail's beauty radiated from light that streamed from Jesus' throne.

A piano plucked flutters of joy over a vast shore before me.

Gail's voice like an angel, filled my soul.

Somewhere over the rainbow, the dreams that you dare to dream really do come true.

A shore stretched for miles, rocks jutted up like fortresses in the sea.

I flowed into the music with dreams of Gail and calm came over me, soothing the war in my heart.

Gail offered me her arms. . .and I flowed into her. . .and all she dreamed about, all she longed for, and the warmth of her flesh with mine became all I dreamed about and all I longed for into a oneness with her I'd never known before.

My heart lapped on the shore. I closed my eyes and soaked in a fading sun, while a breeze passed over my heart.

A sun shimmered through layers of streaks, iridescent on the horizon. Jesus glowed on the horizon over the vast sea.

Made in the USA
Middletown, DE
10 April 2021